Fishing

Though the bulk of the world's fish is caught by large modern fleets, small fishing villages, like this one in Ghana, still exist to supply local needs and a living for the people.

WAYS OF LIFE

Fishing

BY BRIAN WILLIAMS

Illustrated by Bernard Robinson

RAINTREE
Steck-Vaughn
PUBLISHERS
The Steck-Vaughn Company

Austin, Texas

© Copyright 1993, text, Steck-Vaughn Company

All rights reserved. No part of this book may be reproduced or utilized in any form or by any means, electronic or mechanical, including photocopying, recording, or by any information storage and retrieval system, without permission in writing from the Publisher. Inquiries should be addressed to:
Copyright Permissions,
Steck-Vaughn Company,
P.O. Box 26015,
Austin, TX 78755

Published by Raintree Steck-Vaughn Publishers, an imprint of Steck-Vaughn Company

Designed and produced by AS Publishing

Library of Congress Cataloging-in-Publication Data
Williams, Brian, 1943–
    Fishing / by Brian Williams ; illustrated by Bernard Robinson.
        p.   cm. — (Ways of life)
    Includes index.
    Summary: Discusses fishing and the fishing industry around the world, from tuna hunting to the lake fishers of Africa.
    ISBN 0-8114-4788-X
    1. Fisheries—Juvenile literature.   2. Fishing villages—Juvenile literature.   3. Fishers—Juvenile literature.   [1. Fisheries.]   I. Robinson, Bernard, 1930–   ill.   II. Title.   III. Series.
SH331.15.W54   1993
639.2—dc20   92-21389
                                                                              CIP AC

Typeset by Tom Fenton Studio, Neptune, NJ
Printed in Italy by L.E.G.O. s.p.a., Vicenza
Bound in the United States by Lake Book, Melrose Park, IL

1 2 3 4 5 6 7 8 9 0 LB 98 97 96 95 94 93

Cover credits: Hutchison Library (center), San Francisco Tourist Office

Picture credits: Florida Division of Tourism 32/33; Hutchison Library 2, 8, 10, 12, 14, 15, 16, 18, 19 (top), 26, 27, 29, 34, 35, 36/37, 39, 40/41, 42, 45, 47; The Mansell Collection 19 (bottom); Peter Newark's American Pictures 20; San Francisco Tourist Office 44/45.

Contents

FAMILIES OF THE SEA 6

THE BUSINESS OF FISHING 12

FISHING AROUND THE WORLD 21
    Fishing off North America 24
    Trawlers of the North Sea 26
    Iceland and the Cod War 27
    Fishers of the Far North 28
    Northwest Native Americans 30
    Fishing in the South 32
    The Fish-loving Japanese 34
    The Tuna Hunters 35
    Fishing in Asia 36
    Lake Fishers of Africa 38

THE FUTURE FOR FISHING 40

GLOSSARY 46

INDEX 48

FAMILIES OF THE SEA

Ever since people first ventured onto a river or sea in small boats, there have been fishing communities. Those who live by fishing today share many of the same concerns and face the same hazards as those first fishing peoples.

Fishing was one of the first skills that prehistoric people practiced. They learned how to make fishhooks from bone, how to weave fish traps from reeds, and how to make nets from cords made of plant fibers.

Rivers, lakes, and shallow seas provided food all year round. In addition to all kinds of fish, there were oysters, lobsters, crabs, and other kinds of shellfish, and there were seabirds.

Some people fished from the shore with nets and lines. Others waded out to set traps in fast-flowing rivers, and yet more took to boats and paddled away from the shore. Early fishermen used rafts and canoes big enough for only one or two people. Later, they built larger crafts with sails, which could travel farther and carry more people.

Family business

On shore the fishermen's families helped to make nets, lines, ropes, sails, and fish baskets. They cleaned and gutted the fish, cooked it or sold it, or carried it to market. Or they might preserve it for later use by salting, smoking, or drying it.

Everyone in the family had a job, and every family in the community followed much the same way of life. They had the same rewards and shared the same hardships. One day, the waters might teem with fish;

6

Fishing and boat building were skills mastered thousands of years ago by people all around the world. These African lake fishers speared fish from reed boats.

Fishing for food is often best done in groups. Here Chinese workers in a communal fishery draw in their catch.

the next, the fish might be gone. Empty nets could mean starvation for the whole community. So fishermen had to watch and learn the ways of the fish, and they had to make sure that they preserved enough of their catch in good times to tide them over in bad.

In peril on the sea

It took courage to go out in a small canoe or raft, or even in a larger boat. Unknown waters are always dangerous, and the weather can turn a calm sea rough in moments. A single wave can overturn a small boat. Fishermen had to depend on themselves and each other for their safety. They became expert weather forecasters, able to spot the telltale signs of a storm. They kept their boats "ship-shape" so they could lay their hands on a rope or a tool in moments of danger.

Sometimes a whole community might be struck by tragedy. A fleet of fishing boats might disappear in a sudden storm, their crews "missing, presumed drowned." Faced with such troubles, the people turned to their

FISH LORE

Every fishing community has tales and myths of water monsters and spirits.

Changeable gods
The gods of the sea, such as the Greeks' Poseidon (Roman Neptune) and the Polynesians' Tangaroa, were powerful figures in mythology. Fishermen, who made their living from the sea, were especially fearful of the gods' swiftly changing moods.

Indian fish god
In India, Hindus believe that Manu, the ancestor of all humans, was saved from drowning in the Great Flood by a fish whose life he had once spared. It was later revealed the fish was the god Vishnu.

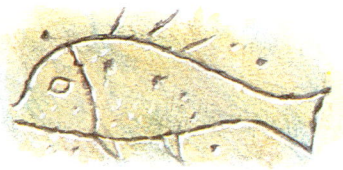

Fishers of men
The Bible tells us much about the fishing community in the days of Jesus. Several of his disciples were fishermen and two of his miracles concern fish. Peter's empty net comes up so full of fish that it almost sinks his boat. And five thousand people are fed from five loaves and two fishes. The fish became a Christian secret symbol during the persecution of the early church.

The kraken
Norwegian fishermen lived in fear of the mythical kraken—a huge dark monster that may well have been a giant squid.

The Loch Ness monster
It was fishermen who first told tales of this prehistoric beast which is said to lurk mysteriously in a peaceful Scottish lake.

Mermaids
Fishermen claim to have seen half-human sea creatures with the head and body of a woman and the tail of a fish, but none was ever caught. It was probably manatees, or sea cows, that they saw feeding their young. The lonely fishermen were probably longing for some female company.

No farewell
Even today, fishing people cling to many old beliefs and superstitions. For example, a well-wisher must not wish a departing fishing crew "good luck," or it will catch nothing.

Fruit for spirits
The fishermen of the tropics still make offerings to sea spirits before a fishing trip. In Senegal, West Africa, fishermen offer gifts of milk and fruit to the sea spirits before they set off on a fishing trip.

God be with them
Priests still bless nets at the start of the fishing season in some parts of the world and hold services to bless the local fishing fleet before it leaves port.

French fears
In fishing villages on the coast of northwest France, wives hung bunches of leeks from the roof beams before the fishermen left home for the long voyage across the North Atlantic to the Grand Banks. If the leeks sprouted, all would be well, but if they withered and died, the family feared the worst.

A fishy start in life
French mothers put their babies to sleep in fish baskets instead of cradles to bring them good luck in later life.

Fruitful partnership
Scottish fishermen would collect a jar of seawater and seaweed from the shore. The water was sprinkled on the cottage floor, and the seaweed hung from the roof. This was to show the people's partnership with the sea—and, it was hoped, ensure a safe return with bulging nets.

No turnover
The Chinese believe that it is unlucky to turn a fish over on your plate while you are eating. They think this means a fishing boat will capsize at sea.

Fisherman's friend
Offerings to sea gods were mostly made to save fishermen from drowning. But not all fishing communities were fearful of the sea. Some saw the ocean as a bountiful friend of humans. An offering was a gift of thanks.

gods for aid. Many believed that the waters were inhabited by spirits, good and evil. They offered prayers and gifts to these spirits, seeking protection against wind and wave, and monsters of the deep.

The industry today

Today fishing has become an industry. A few fishing peoples carry on centuries-old fishing methods, with hand nets, harpoons, and canoes. But most now use outboard motors and diesel engines in place of sails and paddles. Most of the fish we eat today are caught by

modern fishing boats, which are like floating factories. Instead of isolated small communities, whole nations base the major part of their economic life on fishing. The chief fishing nations, such as Japan and Russia, send their fleets all over the world.

Fishing is big business but it still has its problems. Some fishing grounds have been ruined by pollution. Some kinds of fish have become scarce because too many have been caught. Increasing mechanization has meant that fewer jobs are available. Nations continually dispute each others' right to fish how and where they

On a beach in Sri Lanka in the Indian Ocean, fishermen coil their nets to dry, ready for the next day's fishing.

SAFETY AT SEA

Once there was nothing the community ashore could do to help those in trouble at sea. Now ships are in radio contact all the time, receiving weather forecasts and accurate storm warnings. Nevertheless, fishing is still hazardous, especially in the freezing cold waters of the North Atlantic. Every year trawlers are lost. Some are quite small and vulnerable not only to stormy seas but to ice. A ship covered in ice becomes top-heavy and can easily capsize.

Today an air-sea search is swiftly organized to look for a ship in trouble. Survivors must be rescued quickly, for a person cannot live more than a few minutes in such bitterly cold seas.

wish. And, despite modern technology, fishing is still a perilous business.

Every year fishermen are lost at sea. Wives and children wait at home while the boats are away. Sometimes a boat fails to return. The whole community will grieve with the widows and children, but other boats will go out again.

The Business of Fishing

Millions of people are employed in catching, preserving, and selling fish. Millions more of us eat it — fresh, frozen, or canned — thanks to a complicated network of skills and processes that bring it to our table.

Below left: In India people examine the day's catch. In hot countries fresh fish must be sold quickly before it spoils.

FISHING METHODS

Lines
In the shallow waters of the Grand Banks off Newfoundland, fishermen catch cod on long lines. The seabed is rocky and would tear any net. The main lines are miles long with several thousand hooks dangling from them.

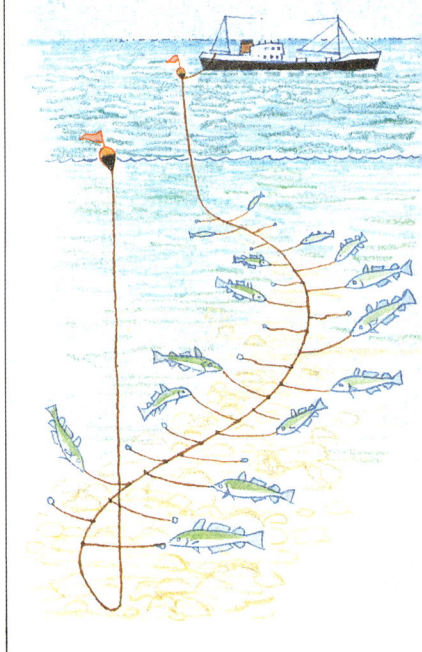

Fish are a particularly valuable food because they are rich in protein. Fish caught 200 nautical miles off the coast belong to nobody until they are caught, and they can be preserved in many ways.

Fish form an important part of the diet of some peoples. The Japanese eat far more fish than meat. So do the Icelanders. Parts of the fish that cannot be eaten, such as the head, tail, fins, and bones, are ground up for use as fertilizer or cattle feed.

Among the most valuable food fish are cod, tuna, haddock, mackerel, salmon, herring, and sardines. Catching these different species requires different techniques. Catching shellfish such as shrimps, mussels, oysters, and lobsters requires still different methods.

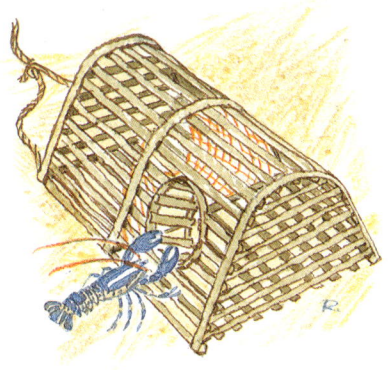

A lobster about to be trapped in a lobster pot. Lured by the bait inside, the lobster cannot find its way out again.

Nets

Most fish are caught in nets. These were once small and made by hand. Today they are huge and made in factories.

A trawl is a bag-shaped net that is dragged along the sea bottom to catch bottom-dwelling fish. Large trawls are hauled by stern trawlers about 230 feet long. Side trawlers are about half as big. Their trawls are trailed over the side rather than the stern (end) of the ship.

Gill nets are like curtains hanging in the water; the fish are trapped in the mesh by their gills. Some gill nets stretch for many miles and trap not just fish but also seabirds, turtles, and dolphins. This "wall of death" fishing is terribly destructive to wildlife and is wasteful since it also kills many fish that are too small to be eaten. Gill nets are now used only illegally.

The seine, or purse, net is drawn around a huge school of fish and then closed, like a pouch, by hauling in lines.

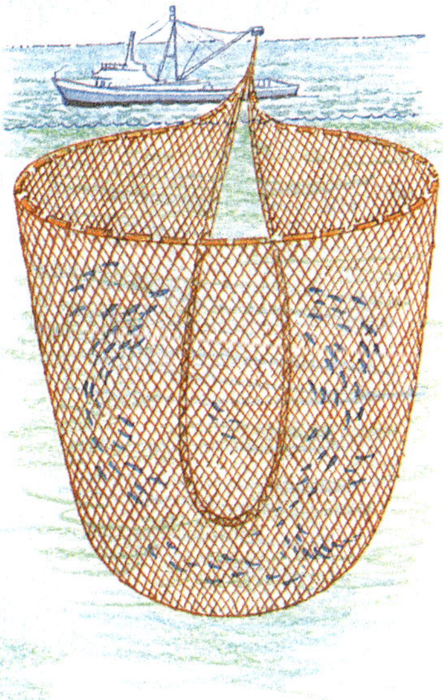

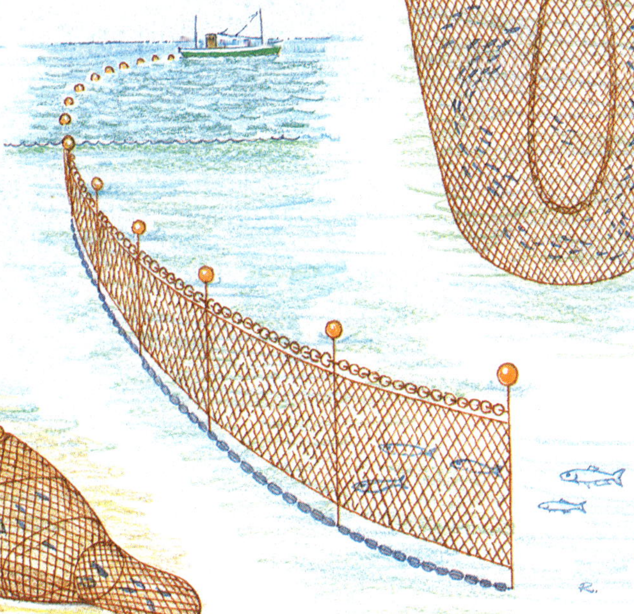

TYPES OF FISH

Freshwater fish live in rivers and lakes, which, unlike the sea, are not salty. Trout are fished commercially, but most freshwater fish are fished only for sport.

Saltwater fish live in the sea, though some, such as salmon, live some of the time in fresh water. Cod, herring, sardines, mackerel, and tuna are important food fishes. Flatfish, such as flounder and halibut, live on the seabed.

Tropical fish live in warm waters and are mostly colorful creatures. The most exotic ones are beautiful to look at but usually less good to eat.

Shellfish are not fish at all according to zoologists. Lobsters, crabs, prawns, and shrimps are crustaceans. Mussels, clams, and squid are mollusks.

Hauling in the net may bring an unwelcome surprise. These Indian fishermen have caught venomous sea snakes as well as fish in their net.

Fishing by day and night

All fishermen know the best times of year to fish and the best places to look for fish. Besides this store of local knowledge, they now have modern aids such as radar and sonar (echolocation) to help track down schools of fish.

Some inland fishermen do not use boats. They set their nets across a river or wade into the shallows at the edge of a lake. For many fishermen, however, the day begins when they make their boat ready. Often the skipper is the boat owner, and he is helped by one or two crewmen. Women are seldom found on small fishing boats, although women do work on large factory ships and ashore.

Back on shore the last fish are shaken out as the net is folded. Young fishermen of tomorrow watch with interest.

Large fishing boats with refrigeration facilities may stay at sea for weeks or months. A small boat usually stays at sea for about a day. Sometimes, the fishing is done at night, when fish come close to the surface to feed. The crew hangs lights above the water to attract the fish.

Hauling in the catch

On board, everyone has to work hard when the nets are ready to be hauled in. On a boat like a trawler, each member of the crew has a job to do. The winches groan, the lines tighten, and — if the crew is lucky — the net comes in, bulging with fish. The crew then sorts through the catch. They throw back fish that are too small or not good to eat.

Fish does not stay fresh for long unless it is iced. In hot climates it must be eaten or sold the day it is caught, so the fishing boats head for home as fast they can. In cooler climates, ships can stay at sea longer, returning to shore with their holds crammed with fish, iced or salted to keep them edible.

Bringing the harvest home

Some fishing communities have no harbors, and instead the boats are hauled up onto the beach. People from the village run to help the crews unload the fish they have caught.

Much of the fish is eaten by local people. Some is sold in the market, and the rest is processed. Today on board a modern fishing boat, the fish are cleaned and packed as

Drying fish in the sun in Angola, Africa. Drying is a simple and cheap way to preserve fish for eating later.

FISH FESTIVITIES

Just as farmers celebrate the harvest from the land, fishing communities celebrate the sea's harvest.

Oyster Feast
In the English town of Colchester an Oyster Feast is hosted by the mayor. The town has enjoyed oyster-fishing rights on the Colne River since 1186, and the mayor takes a trip in a fishing boat each year to reassert those ancient rights.

Clambake
The Native Americans in New England cooked and ate clams fresh from the sea. They taught the settlers how to bake them (below). They lit a charcoal fire in the sandy beach and heated rocks. Then they spread the rocks with a layer of seaweed and a layer of clams—and maybe corn on the cob and potatoes. On top went another layer of seaweed. The heat from the rocks and the water from the seaweed steamed the clams to perfection. Clambake parties are still a feature of New England life.

Frozen festival
Crawfish are popular in Scandinavia where they were traditionally fished from rivers. Swedish people even decorate their homes with pictures of crawfish and celebrate the crawfish season with parties in August each year. Hopeful fishermen go out in boats at night and use lanterns to attract the crawfish, which they scoop up in baskets. But crawfish are no longer plentiful in Sweden. They are imported frozen, mostly from the United States.

Native Americans show the settlers how to bake clams.

Another satisfied customer. Here in India, as in many fishing countries, local catches are sold on the beach.

soon as they are caught. But in the past women gutted and cleaned the fish, working at the wharf with nimble fingers and sharp knives. It was cold, tiring, and monotonous work. The fish were then packed into boxes, sold in the port, and sent by road or rail to the towns. Fresh fish has to be transported quickly, or it will not reach market in prime condition.

In the market

Fishermen hope for large catches of fish. However, if there is too much fish for sale, the market price falls. The skippers will get less money, and there will be less profit to share with the crew. If fish are scarce, the men have to work harder to fill the holds. But the price at auction will be higher, so the rewards will be greater for the lucky skipper who comes in with a good catch.

Fish markets are run by auctioneers. The fish is

FULTON FISH MARKET

Every weekday morning South Street in New York City comes alive with the activity of the Fulton Fish Market. The fish market began in 1831 as part of the Fulton Market. It was operated by local fish dealers as a public city market and has supplied the New York metropolitan area with fresh fish for many years. The market has always been a lively place full of people, fish, and strong smells.

The Fulton Fish Market operates in much the same way that it did in the 1800s. Fish were delivered by boat until the 1950s. Today the fish are flown in and delivered by truck. Trucks carrying fish arrive between 12:00 AM and 1:00 AM and unload until about 2 AM. The market is open from midnight to 9:00 AM Monday through Friday and is busiest at 3:30 AM.

Above: Buyers inspect the fish in Tokyo's fish market, while the auctioneer talks up the price.

In Britain fishwives—women who sold fish on the street—were notorious for their "scolding tongues" and "shrewish tempers." They led very hard lives which no doubt accounted for their ill tempers.

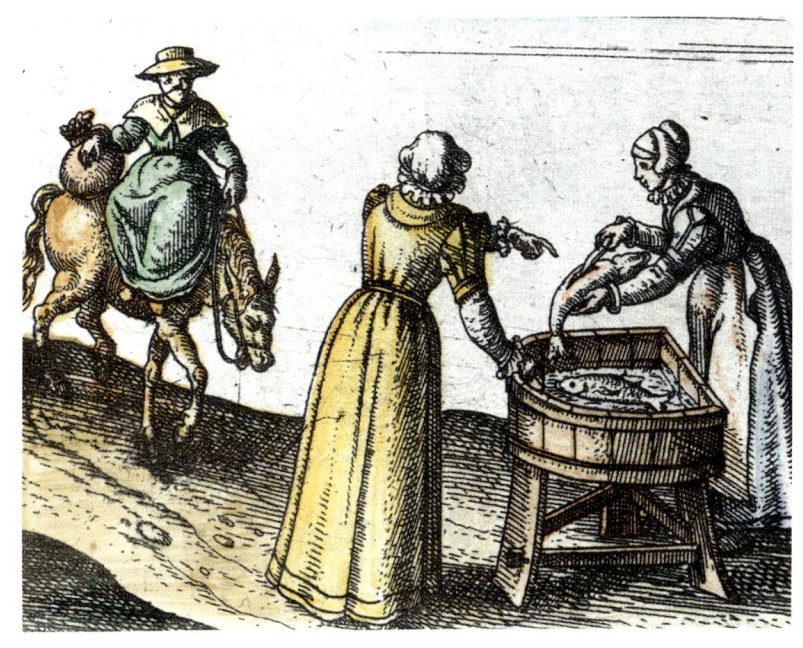

usually displayed in boxes. Buyers inspect the fish before deciding what to buy. The auctioneer tries to encourage the buyers to bid a high price. He may run a Dutch auction, starting the price high and lowering it until one of the buyers agrees to buy.

While the fishermen rest, the fish is speeding to processing plants, food stores, and restaurants. The catch hauled out of a cold sea on a dark night ends up as fish neatly packaged in a supermarket or elegantly served on a restaurant dish.

WHALES

Whales are mammals not fish. They have been hunted since ancient times. Whalers from many countries made long voyages to find the great beasts. They then took to small boats and used harpoons to kill them. The dead whales were towed back to the main ship to be butchered for meat and oil. The whaling industry was at its peak in the nineteenth century. All along the coast of New England, there were whaling ports from which ships like this one (below) set sail. In the 1920s whaling factory ships came into use. They were so efficient that whale stocks declined alarmingly. Small boats with exploding harpoons caught the whales. A huge blue whale could be hauled on board and cut up for boiling in 45 minutes. Today we no longer need whale products, and conservationists are fighting to protect the last whales from the countries that persist in hunting them.

American whalers hunting in the 1850s.

Fishing Around the World

The shores of every continent have become home to fishing communities. Every ocean and great lake have fishing settlements, many of them ancient ones that in the past had little contact with neighbors inland. Few such traditional communities exist today, but people all around the world still depend on fish for their living.

The world's great fishing grounds are the North Atlantic near Iceland and Newfoundland, the north Pacific near Japan and Russia, and the eastern Pacific off South and Central America. The countries bordering these fishing grounds—Japan, Russia, China, the United States, Chile, and Peru—have the largest fishing industries and some of the oldest fishing communities.

Nearly 90 percent of the world's fishing catch is taken from the sea. The rest comes from rivers, lakes, streams, and onshore fish farms. China, India, and Russia have the biggest onshore fishing industries.

A traditional fisherman can feed his family without destroying fish stocks. Huge factory ships scoop up the schools of fish, leaving the ocean a desert.

Where fish flourish

The Grand Banks is a stretch of shallow water about 500 miles long off the coast of Newfoundland in the Atlantic Ocean. These waters are cold and full of nutrients, just right for cod. That is why they have been a magnet for fishermen for so long. They have been fished since the 1400s when men from Britain and France braved the Atlantic waves in small sailing boats.

The shallow waters all the way down the coast of New England are crowded with fish. Cod, herring, pollack, whiting, flounder, lobsters, and shellfish are found there.

The map shows the world's most heavily fished seas and general fishing areas. Most fish are caught close to the land where they are most plentiful. Thanks to international cooperation, fish stocks that were declining in the 1960s and 1970s are now recovering.

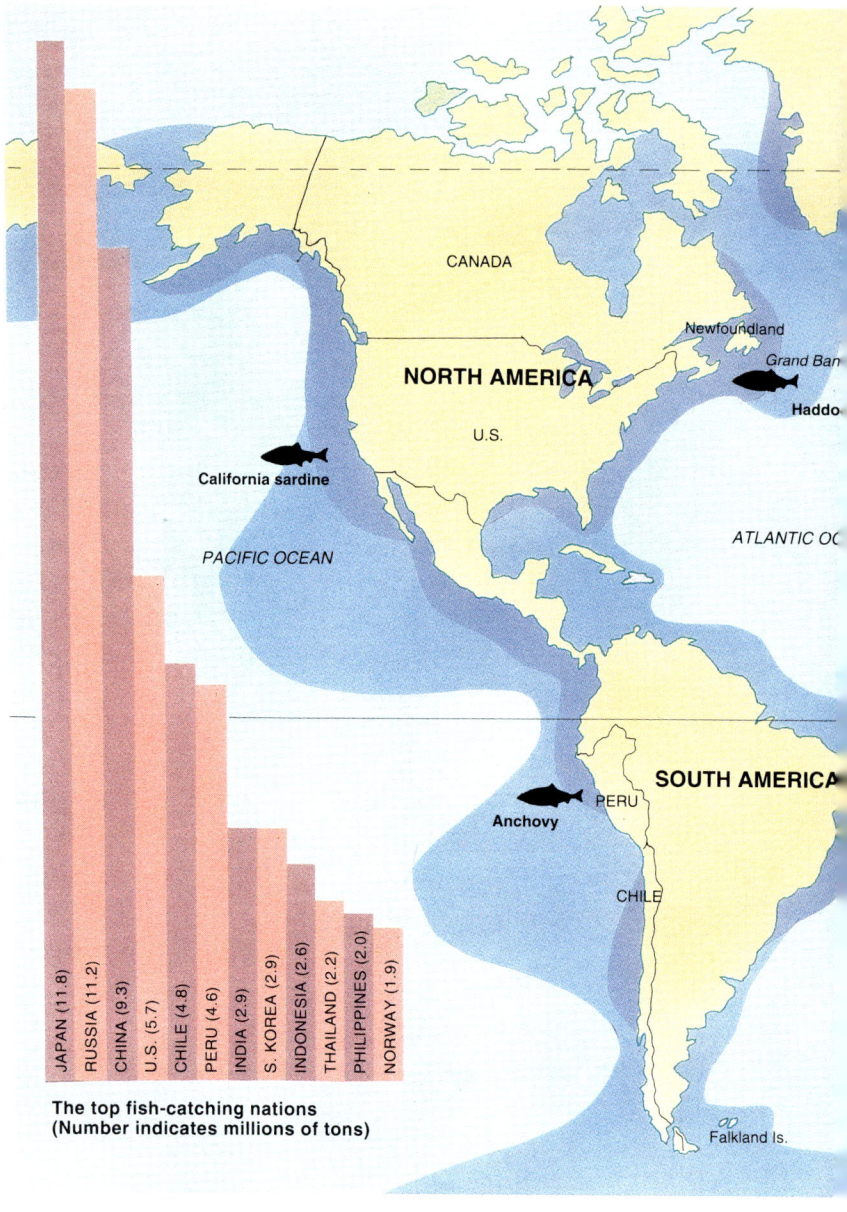

The top fish-catching nations
(Number indicates millions of tons)

JAPAN (11.8), RUSSIA (11.2), CHINA (9.3), U.S. (5.7), CHILE (4.8), PERU (4.6), INDIA (2.9), S. KOREA (2.9), INDONESIA (2.6), THAILAND (2.2), PHILIPPINES (2.0), NORWAY (1.9)

North America
Canada, the United States, and Mexico all have large fishing industries. Fishing boats ply the Atlantic, the Gulf of Mexico, and the Pacific Ocean. Inuit and other Native Americans fish traditional areas, and historic fishing grounds like Newfoundland and Nova Scotia have ancient fishing communities. There are large fish farm businesses and much lake fishing for sport.

South America
Chile and Peru are South America's chief fishing countries. Much of the catch comes from the waters of the cold, food-rich Peru Current off the west coast of the continent. The southern waters toward Antarctica are also rich fishing grounds. There is important inland fishing in lakes and rivers, especially in the Amazon region.

Europe
Europe has a very long coastline, and fishing communities can be found from the cold Arctic to the warm Mediterranean. Leading fishing nations in Europe include Russia, Norway, Iceland, Spain, France, Poland, and Britain.

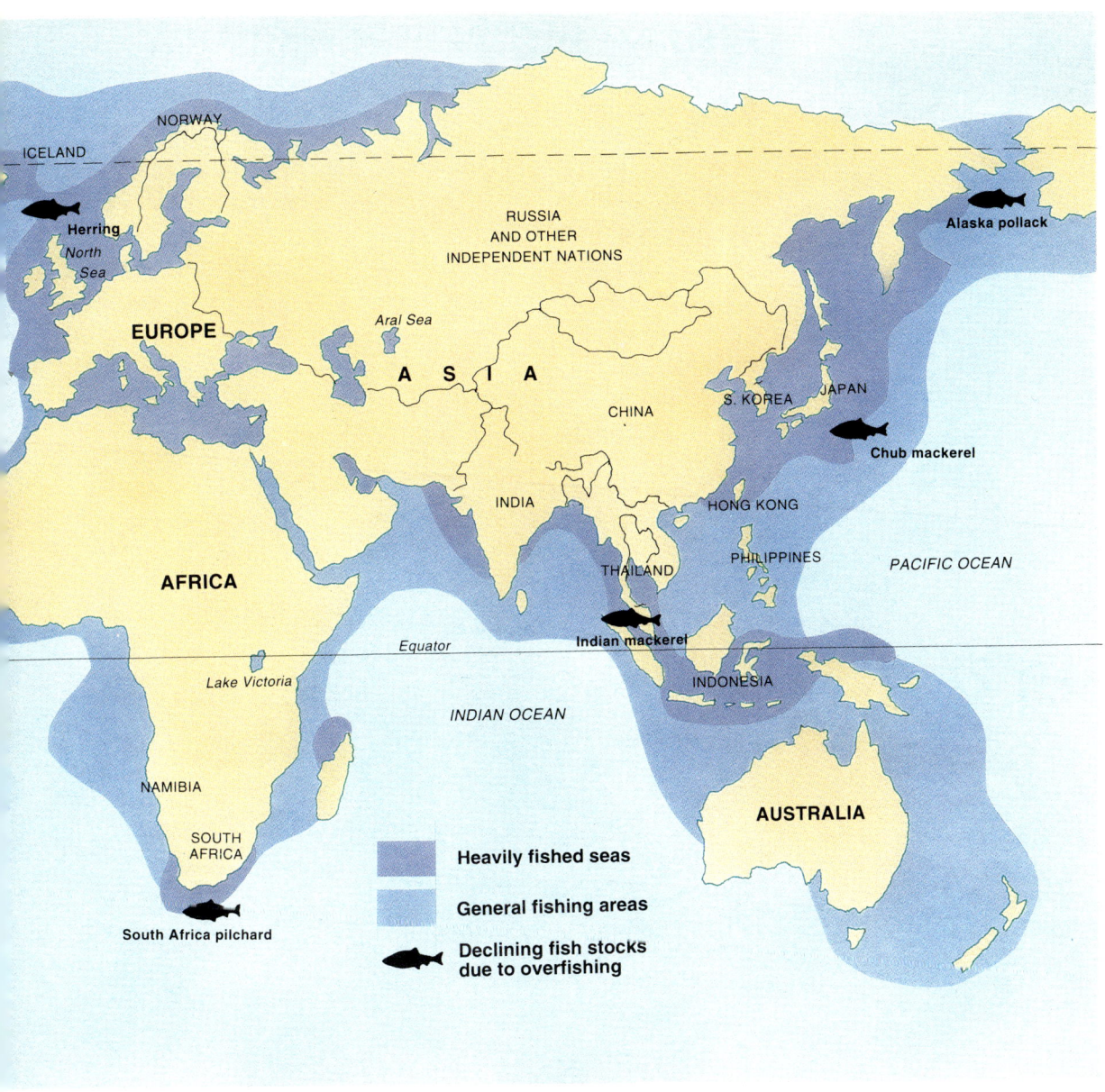

Africa
Many Africans living in coastal regions fish for food, mostly in small boats. People in lake and riverside communities catch fish in natural waterways and also in man-made lakes such as Lake Volta. Some countries, such as Namibia and South Africa, operate sea fishing fleets and have fish canning industries.

Asia
Fish is an important part of the diet of many Asians. Japan is the world's leading fish-catching nation, while China leads the world in fish farm production. In the Far East and Southeast Asia many people live in waterside villages and fish from small craft. India, South Korea, Indonesia, and Thailand have many fishing communities.

Australia
In Australia, New Zealand, and the Pacific Islands much fishing is done by people working alone or in small groups. Many islanders depend on fishing for food. Australia and New Zealand have growing fishing industries, although the people in these countries do not themselves eat a great deal of fish.

FISHING OFF NORTH AMERICA

The harvesting of the sea was vital to the settlement of America. The colonists could scarcely have survived without fish. They copied the Indians' method of erecting nets on stakes to snare fish to eat and learned from them how to use fish as fertilizer. The land was rocky, so they could not farm it successfully, but the forests provided plentiful timber with which to build ships. Beginning in the mid-1700s the settlers built sailing ships to catch fish and to carry cargoes of dried and salted fish to Europe and the West Indies.

Hauling in his catch from the Grand Banks, this nineteenth-century fisherman worked from dawn to fill his flat-bottomed dory. At dusk he rowed back with the other boats to the schooner.

On the Grand Banks

The traditional fishing method was from a large sailing schooner. Banks-fishing schooners were first used in the 1800s. These two-masted vessels of about 100 tons carried small rowboats, called "dories," stacked inside one another. The crew took to these boats when they reached the fishing grounds.

The men's working day began at sunrise. Each man had his own dory with hooks, long lines, and bait. Each would fish until his dory was full and then return to the schooner, the fleet's mother ship. It was hard work from dawn to dusk, but the Grand Banks seldom failed to provide the crews with holds full of fish.

SACRED COD

A Sacred Cod, 5 feet long and carved from a block of pine, hangs in the Massachusetts State House. Cod fishing was so important to the people of the Massachusetts Bay Colony in the 1700s that they exempted fishermen from military service.

Trawlers of the North Sea

For centuries European communities have depended on the North Sea fishing grounds for their livelihoods. Until the mid-1900s many people did not eat meat on Fridays or during Lent, so fish was an important part of their diet.

The men who live and work on deep-sea trawlers today often have to endure extremes of cold, when their boats steam into the northern oceans. Good catches of cod, haddock, and other fish are to be found in these waters, but it is a tough life, filled with danger. Stormy seas, fog, icebergs, and ice buildup on the ship are just some of the ever-present threats.

Ship's company

About eight people, usually men, make up the crew of a small trawler. They have to live and work together for days on end in a confined space. They rely entirely on each other's skills, fortitude, and good humor. The skipper is in charge: He is the navigator, and he decides where to fish. The engineer sees that the engine keeps running, and the cook prepares large meals for the hungry crew. In the freezing cold waters of the Arctic a human body needs plenty of energy to keep working.

The trawler maintains contact at all times with the land and with other vessels by radio. Sophisticated equipment helps to avoid hazards, but accidents do occur. In an emergency, there is a chance of rescue, but hands on the trawler know that their safety is best protected by their own vigilance. Their families become accustomed to living without them for weeks on end and in the fear that they may not return at all.

Low wages for the workers

The companies that own the fishing fleets make considerable profits, but the workers at sea and in the processing industry are relatively low-paid. Because of fishing limits and agreed-on quotas, the boats go out less often, so jobs at sea are hard to get. The deckhands, who are paid per trip rather than a weekly wage, earn less and less. Fishermen are forced to leave the sea and look for jobs on shore. Life affords few luxuries and little security for the fishing communities of the North Sea and the northeastern Atlantic.

Above: At the dock in Mallaig, hardy fishermen of the northern Scottish Isles unload a harvest of the cold gray Atlantic. The fish will be frozen and transported by road to the large population centers to the south in Scotland and England.

Right: Trawlermen at Whitby in northeast England follow a long tradition of seamanship. But the demand for wet fish has declined so much that the fishing fleets are becoming less and less profitable.

Iceland and the Cod War

Iceland is an island in the North Atlantic with a population of only 250,000. The land is too cold for growing crops other than hay to feed livestock. The Icelanders depend on fish. Most of them live in coastal towns and work in the fishing industry.

Almost all of Iceland's exports are of fish and fish products. They have to sell enough fish to pay for consumer goods, virtually all of which were once imported. Today, with the help of overseas aid and investment, Iceland is developing industries, but fishing is still vital.

Banning the British

The Icelandic waters once teemed with fish and were traditionally fished by other European countries, especially Britain. But with stocks of fish, especially cod, being depleted, the Icelanders grew worried and banned other nations from its waters. Each time Iceland extended its fishing limits, Britain objected.

In 1975 Iceland imposed a 230-mile fishing limit, which was disregarded by British fishing vessels. Icelandic gunboats patrolled the seas to chase off foreign trawlers. Britain sent its navy to protect its fishing boats but in the end agreed to abide by the limit. The cod war was over.

Summer was an easier time for the Arctic peoples than winter. Here children listen to a singer while fish dry on poles at the watery edge, a seal skin is staked out to dry, a fisherman casts his net from a kayak, and small whales line the shore ready to be cut up.

FISHERS OF THE FAR NORTH

The Inuit of the Arctic developed a way of life totally dependent on hunting and fishing. Almost all their food came from the ocean or from rivers because no crops could grow in the frozen Arctic soil.

The Inuit lived in partnership with the ocean. Their boats were the skin-covered umiak and smaller kayak, and in them they paddled between the ice floes on hunting trips. The water in the Arctic is so cold that a person would die in minutes if he or she fell in. In the summer, the Inuit netted fish in the rivers. In the winter, when the ocean froze, they cut holes through the ice to fish or hunt seals with harpoons.

Endless night and endless day

During the Arctic winter, when it is dark for most of the day, Inuit families kept to their homes. They spent what time they could making new weapons and sleds, harnesses for their dogs, and clothes from furs. They also carved in bone and ivory, working by the light of oil lamps.

A more sociable life returned with the sun in spring. After fishing or hunting, people would gather for a shared meal. They told stories and jokes. Everyone shared food, for in this harsh world of snow and ice, such hospitality is vital.

Inuit life today

Since the 1800s, life for the Arctic peoples has changed. Many have given up old beliefs and become Christians and have also given up some ancient customs. Instead of wandering with their tents, people now live in houses. Instead of hunting and fishing, they work in the oil and mining industries.

The modern world has brought problems for the Inuit, such as unemployment and alcoholism. Inuit leaders have tried to keep alive the many native languages. They encourage the teaching of traditional skills, such as how to build an igloo or paddle a kayak, to children who also watch television and read comics. These children will never know the old way of life, but perhaps they will retain the old sense of community.

Right: Today tents and skin boats are no more. They have been replaced by drab modern housing and outboard motors. It is difficult for people to keep the old ways alive.

Northwest Native Americans

The ocean off the northwest coast of America swarms with wildlife, including whales, halibut, herring, salmon, and candlefish. Native Americans such as the Chinook and Tlingit lived here long before European settlers first explored the Pacific coast and made full use of its riches.

The king of fish was the salmon. The Indians trapped salmon in weirs (dams) built across the rivers where the fish swam to spawn. Herring, too, were so plentiful in the breeding season that people with wooden rakes could scoop fish from the water. The candlefish was so full of oil that it burned like a candle when dried. Nobody ever went hungry. Northwest Native Americans fished only during the summer. The winter was spent in leisure activities.

Leisure and luxury

Because the necessities of life came easily, the Indians had enough time to develop other skills. They built timber homes and carved elaborate totem poles to stand outside them. They wove blankets and baskets with

The regular return of salmon to their river spawning grounds guarantees good fishing for local people.

Native Americans of the northwest coast at a potlatch. Every guest received a gift, for generosity was the mark of a successful chief.

beautiful patterns. They carved pots and dishes for their own use and to give as gifts. They made masks to represent spirits and animals. They made pipes from stone and bone, and beat copper into dishes and knives. They made great seagoing canoes large enough for 50 men. Many people grew wealthy, especially when the Europeans arrived to trade with them.

Giving and taking

In northwest Indian society chiefs ruled and had the right to the best fishing grounds. Cedarwood houses faced the sea and were so big that many families lived in each one. Slaves (often people captured in war) could be badly treated and sometimes even sacrificed in rites to mark the launch of a new canoe. Chiefs displayed their wealth by giving great parties known as potlatches at which gifts were distributed to all the guests.

Today tourists admire the craft work of the Indians. Some of the Indians still earn their living from fishing and running or working in salmon canneries, but there is little left of their traditional way of life.

The Indians erected weirs like this one across rivers. As the salmon traveled upstream, they were caught by the hundreds.

FISHING IN THE SOUTH

Florida, almost surrounded by water, has a thriving fishing industry. There are more kinds of fish in and around Florida than anywhere else in the world. In the ocean waters fishermen catch tuna, mackerel, mullet, red snapper, sea trout, and other food fish, as well as shark and menhaden (a kind of herring), which are processed into fertilizers, oil, and food for livestock. In the rivers and lakes they catch bass, bream, and freshwater trout. The waters of the Gulf of Mexico contain large quantities of shrimps, lobsters, and other shellfish.

Traditionally the shellfish were caught in snares or pots, but now they are mostly caught by trawl nets. Fewer and fewer people go out in small shrimp boats, and fewer people are needed to work the bigger boats. Former fishermen and their families now work in the tourist industry. Fishing skippers earn extra money by

Tourists visiting the coast of Florida can buy exotic sponges like these. So many sponges are being collected and sold that some kinds of sponges are now quite rare.

SHRIMPS

Catching shrimps is big business in many countries. In the United States, shrimps are caught in Florida, Louisiana, Texas, and in the cold waters off Alaska. Shrimps are also caught in Mexico and in several Asian countries including Thailand and Indonesia.

HURRICANES

Today fishermen are given advance warning of approaching hurricanes, but once they had to rely on their own skill and experience to know when to batten down the hatches and head for home.

SPONGES

Fishermen do not only catch fish. Sponges thrive in the warm waters off Florida's coasts. In shallow waters, fishermen use glass-bottomed boats to locate them. Then they fish them out of the water with a hook on a pole. In deeper water they dive for them. At one time the fishermen simply held their breath, cut the sponges, and came up for air. Today they wear scuba diving gear.

taking tourists for boat trips around the islands that make up the Florida Keys.

Crawfishing

Crawfish are like small lobsters. They live in fresh water in lakes and rivers rather than in the ocean. They are just as good to eat as lobsters and were always popular in fishing communities in Europe. They were hardly eaten at all in America. Now the state of Louisiana produces more crawfish than anywhere else in the world. The crawfish are raised on fish farms.

Restaurants in this part of the United States are famed for their fish dishes, such as blackened redfish and seafood gumbo, a soup thickened with okra that originated in Africa. Fish and fishing are very much a part of Louisiana life. The people enjoy two annual festivals to celebrate seafood: a crab festival in June and a shrimp festival in September.

The freshwater crawfish is smaller than its cousin, the saltwater lobster. In the United States crawfish are raised on fish farms.

THE FISH-LOVING JAPANESE

The people of Japan eat more fish than meat. Nowhere in Japan is much more than 60 miles from the ocean. The country has more than 3,000 islands. The land is mountainous and difficult to farm. Until this century the people were mostly poor. They relied on the free harvest of the ocean.

Today the Japanese have more fishing vessels and catch more fish than any other nation, more than twice as much as the United States. They catch salmon, tuna, sardines, mackerel, squid, crabs, and many exotic species. Their fishing boats are the most up-to-date in the world, and they fish virtually all over the world. They also have many fish farms and oyster beds.

PEARLS

Once Japanese women spent several hours a day diving for oysters. If they were lucky, they might find an oyster with a pearl in it. If not, they would have oysters to eat and maybe enough to sell. The pearl fishers had no breathing apparatus. They dived to the seabed, put as many oysters as they could in their small nets, and hoped to surface before they ran out of breath. Later the Japanese discovered how to produce cultured pearls.

FRESH FROM THE WATER

The Japanese like their fish fresh. They often eat it raw, and fish dealers usually taste the raw flesh of fish in the market before they agree to buy it. Restaurants serve "sushi," cold rice with a selection of raw fish and seaweed.

A colorful display of fish in Japan. The Japanese eat a lot of fish, including many kinds unfamiliar to diners in North America and Europe.

34

The Tuna Hunters

Tuna are an important food fish. Tuna are hunters, following the smaller fish on which they feed. They arrive at certain places in great numbers at the same times every year. Because of their great speed and immense size—up to 13 feet long and weighing up to 1,100 pounds—they are prized by sports fishers. The Japanese are the main commercial catchers and consumers of tuna. They net more than three times as much tuna as the United States. Off the Pacific coasts of the United States and Canada, tuna are caught by trolling.

Tuna are powerful fish with a fighting spirit, and catching them has never been easy. Mediterranean fishermen have caught tuna since ancient times. The fishermen work together to trap and kill them. They encircle a school inside a ring net in shallow water. As the net is drawn tighter, the fishers surround the fish and attack their thrashing bodies with knives and harpoons.

Tuna are big fish to catch on a line. Sports fishing fans are eager to try their luck on board charter boats like this one.

FISHING IN ASIA

The people of Southeast Asia are mostly poor, but the seas around the mainland of China and around the islands of the Pacific are rich in fish. Fish plays an important part in local cooking, as it does in Japan.

Shallow-water fishing and collecting shellfish are ancient skills practiced by skilled sailors in a variety of boats—sampans and junks in the China Seas, *mashwas* in the Indian Ocean, and seagoing canoes in the Pacific Islands. These small craft were driven by paddles or single sails. In the Pacific, outrigger canoes can still be seen, but fishermen all over the region prefer motorboats —if they can afford them.

Hard living on the water

Many people cannot afford a home on land, and on islands like Hong Kong, with its vast population, there is precious little space for them, so they make do with floating homes in the harbors. Thousands of people live in small wooden houseboats or in sampans with a cabin roofed with mats. Many of them hope to make a living or at least feed their families by fishing.

Life is very cramped for these boat people. Even in the wooden boats, five or six people may live, eat, and sleep in a space no bigger than one small room in a suburban Western house. There is little room for furniture, and on hot nights some family members sleep on deck in the open air. Drinking water must be brought from land in plastic bottles or cans. The people buy their groceries and oil for cooking from floating shops, small motorboats crammed with goods that chug around the houseboats jammed into the harbor. There are even floating medical clinics and hairdressers.

Finding a new life

This way of life is dying out. The traditional small craft of Asia have sails and cannot compete with modern motor trawlers. The big boats take fish from deep water, which the small boats cannot reach. The shallow inland waters that local people fished for centuries have become exhausted or spoiled by pollution from towns and factories on shore and by waste from the floating homes themselves.

Getting around between the junks in Hong Kong's harbor. In Asia, there are still genuine boat people more at home on the sea than on land.

With no fish to catch, the people cannot wrest a living from the sea. Many fishing people are giving up their waterborne life. Some still live in their houseboats but no longer catch fish for a living. Instead they work on the land in factories and offices. Others have given up the water altogether, and the lucky ones have been rehoused by their governments on land. For people who have spent their whole lives by the sea, learning new skills and adapting to life in a teeming city is often difficult.

LAKE FISHERS OF AFRICA

The great lakes and rivers of central Africa provide a livelihood for the people who live on their shores. Local people use nets and traps to catch fish in the shallows or in rivers. They build a dam of stakes, and from it they hang large basketlike traps. The traps have a wide opening facing upstream and narrow to a closed end. Fish that swim inside are trapped.

Teamwork is found among fishing people all over the world, and the African fishermen often work in teams.

One group makes a bridge of boats across a river at night. They lower nets into the water to make a trap from one side to the other. The rest of the village acts as beaters, wading into the river and driving fish into the trap by beating the water with paddles and sticks.

Threat to lake fish

Lake fish live in a delicate balance of nature, and altering this balance can have disastrous results. In Africa's Lake Victoria, local fishermen used to catch 300 different species of fish. During the 1950s, Nile perch were

Hundreds of spectators line the shore as these Nigerian lake fishers compete to catch the biggest fish during a fishing festival.

The Nile perch is big and good to eat but also fond of eating other fish. An introduced species like this can upset the balance of nature in a lake.

introduced. These fish were large, hungry hunters and ate the smaller fish. Weighing as much as 220 pounds each, the perch also broke the fishermen's nets.

The fishing community had to change its methods. They made stronger nets to catch the Nile perch, and this fish now makes up 70 percent of their catch. A cannery processes Nile perch fillets for export. But smoking the perch requires firewood, and trees are scarce in the area. Also, scientists are not sure what the perch feed on now that most of the small lake fish have been eaten. Perhaps they are cannibals, eating their own young. One day soon the numbers of perch will fall, and then what will happen to the lake fishermen and their economy?

The Future for Fishing

Italian fishermen on the wharf at Pozzuoli near Naples. For thousands of years, people have fished in the Mediterranean Sea, but these fishermen's future is uncertain due to pollution of the water.

In all but the poorest parts of the world, traditional fishing communities will disappear. Our fish will be caught by small crews on huge ships or bred by the thousands on farms. Only those who fish for sport will experience the hazards and joys of fishing.

For hundreds of years the lives of fishing communities around the world did not change. They built boats, made their nets and lines, and then waited for the fish to come in the right season. Mostly, the fish came, though there were bad years when people went hungry. Yet fishing families seldom starved, for the world's oceans were immensely rich.

Fishermen no longer rely on sails and their own instincts to find fish. Now they have motors and radar to help. But their lives are still hard. The modern world has brought many changes, and the people who live by the sea have had to change, too.

In many parts of the world fishermen have two jobs. They fish for part of the year with two or three families sharing the costs of a boat. The rest of the year they may work as engineers, or as wood-carvers making goods to sell to tourists, or as farmers on family-owned land.

Fishing port to tourist resort

Many small fishing ports have become popular tourist resorts. Visitors come in summer, and the money they spend helps the local economy. Tourists gather at the harbor on warm, sunny mornings to watch the fishermen unload their shimmering catches. They enjoy seeing the local people come to purchase their fish on the dock or later in the local market.

Some fishermen lease their boats to sports anglers eager to bring back a big catch. There are stores selling fishing tackle, exotic shells, and souvenirs. Seafood restaurants are kept busy. But when autumn comes, the tourists return to their big cities, and the villagers go back to their normal less colorful life.

Tampering with nature

The world's great irrigation programs have brought many economic benefits, especially to farmers. But they have also caused ecological disasters that have particularly affected fishing communities. Introducing new species of fish to inland waters for supposedly beneficial reasons has also upset the balance of nature.

Once these boats fished in the Aral Sea, but the shrinking of the lake has left them high and dry. The lake's fishing community has simply dried up.

A lake dries up

The Aral Sea in Turkestan is one of the largest inland lakes in the world. The lake once supported a thriving fishing industry. But today the fishermen's boats rot in the sun. They have been stranded as the Aral Sea has shrunk.

The shrinking of the Aral Sea has been caused by huge irrigation programs. The Soviet government built dams to divert the rivers that flowed into the Aral Sea. The water was used to fill canals that watered new cotton fields. Starved of its vital fresh water, the sea has evaporated in the hot sun and become saltier. Since 1960 a third of the Aral Sea has vanished, and the remaining waters are heavily polluted. Fish have died out, and the fishing villages are deserted. This environmental disaster has destroyed a fishing community.

> **THE ALEWIFE'S TALE**
>
> An unforeseen diaster occurred when the St. Lawrence Seaway was opened. Alewives and lampreys suddenly had access to the Great Lakes. The lampreys killed the lake trout and other native species, which might otherwise have killed young alewives and prevented their population from increasing. So might the lampreys. But the Canadian government, in an effort to save the native fish, eradicated the lampreys. Soon the alewife population exploded. Then they in their turn had to be dealt with, and it probably will continue.

Pollution

People use the oceans as a huge dumping ground. They deliberately spill sewage, chemicals, oil, garbage, and even nuclear waste. These upset the balance of marine life and poison millions of fish. The oil spill from the tanker *Exxon Valdez* in 1989 fouled 1,400 square miles of ocean off Alaska, killing marine animals and many fish. Besides accidental disasters, millions of tons of waste oil are deliberately discharged into the sea by tankers flushing their tanks.

Fortunately, efforts are now being made internationally to prevent pollution. The 17 nations that border the Mediterranean, for example, are joining together to clean up the sea before it becomes even more dangerous. And many countries are introducing controls to prevent continued destruction of their rivers and lakes.

Overfishing

Modern fishing methods have meant that hardly any fish can escape the nets, not even the tiny ones. Unless enough fish escape to breed and renew the population, a fish species can quickly become extinct in one area. In the past, fishing fleets simply moved on to scoop up more fish somewhere else.

In the United States, foreign boats are being replaced by American ones, which keeps boat yards busy. The North Pacific fishery is growing rapidly. In Europe, the European Community is trying to encourage fishermen to give up their jobs because there are simply too many boats chasing too few fish. Everyone agrees that with a world hungry for fish and fish products, fishing in the oceans, lakes, and rivers must be properly controlled.

Fishing limits

Many fishing countries now have strict controls over their offshore waters and how the fish there may be caught. Local and foreign fishing boats have to obey quota regulations. They may catch a certain amount of fish in one season—and no more. Nets must have holes large enough to let smaller fish escape. In this way fish stocks can be preserved for the future.

Most countries now impose a 200-nautical mile (230-mile) fishing limit around their coasts. Some fishing countries do not agree with such limits and their boats

Dead fish are often a sign of poisoned water polluted by chemicals such as fertilizers, industrial waste, or (in this case) oil.

try to continue fishing closer to the shore. Both Argentina and Iceland have been in dispute with Britain over fishing zones, and Peru has had difficulty keeping foreign vessels away.

The limits have seriously affected Japan, which has always sent its fishing boats all over the world. Some Japanese fishermen have been forced to give up ocean fishing. They now either fish in Japanese coastal waters or have gone to work on shore.

As real fishing communities disappear, fake ones reappear for the benefit of tourists.

Fisherman's Wharf in San Francisco draws thousands of visitors each year. At one time fish were landed here from fishing boats. Today Fisherman's Wharf is best known for its seafood restaurants.

Below right: Times change, but fishing goes on—here in China, on a fish farm, and around the world.

Fish farming

More and more fish are being reared by intensive methods on farms. Fish such as trout, which were seldom available commercially, are now sold in supermarkets. The Chinese lead the world in farming fish. They have reared carp in ponds since ancient times, and today other species such as salmon are also reared artificially. This means cheaper fish on the supermarket shelves, and sometimes new work for fishing communities.

Tomorrow's world

More than six million people are employed worldwide in the fishing industry today. As ships become more sophisticated, smaller crews are required. But more people are needed to work on land in the processing industry, in fish farming, and in the marketing of fish.

How many of the old fishing communities will still be catching fish in the next century? Probably few of them. More and more fishing ports will be turned into tourist centers with yachts and cruisers replacing the old fishing boats in the harbor. More of the fish we eat will come from farms. Old fishing villages will lie empty and forgotten, like the rusting whaling stations in the Antarctic. But the songs and stories of the fishermen will probably still be told.

Glossary

Anglers People who fish with hook and line.
Auction Sale of goods to the person who bids the highest.
Bait Material that is put on a hook or in a trap to attract fish.
Balance of nature Natural condition in which plants and animals live and interract with each other. It can be upset by the introduction of new species or by changes in the environment.
Breeding season Time of year when a fish mates and produces offspring.
Canals Artificial waterways for transportation or irrigation.
Canneries Factories where fish are canned.
Canoes Small boats propelled by paddles.
Charter boats Boats hired out for fishing trips.
Clambake Method of steaming clams by layering with seaweed over a pit fire.
Colonists Settlers in a new country.
Commercial To do with trade and profit rather than sport or pleasure.
Communal fishery Place where fishing is practiced by people working together for the benefit of the whole community.
Consumer Person who buys a product to eat or use.
Consumer goods Products, other than food, that are used in the home.
Crustaceans Animals with hard shells, such as lobsters and crabs.
Cultured pearls Pearls grown artificially by inserting a grain of sand or some other foreign body into oysters.
Deckhand Person who crews a fishing boat.

Deep-sea fishing Fishing carried out beyond offshore waters, in deeper parts of the ocean.
Dutch auction Auction in which the auctioneer starts with a high price and reduces it until a buyer is found.
Ecological disasters Disasters that adversely affect the environment and the people and wildlife that live in it.
Economy The resources of a community and the use it makes of them.
Factory ship The base ship of a fishing or whaling fleet, where processing of the fish begins.
Fish farm Place where captive fish are raised in enclosed ocean pens or small freshwater ponds until big enough to eat.
Fishing grounds Areas of the ocean where fish are found in abundance.
Fishing limits Extent of an area or zone of ocean around a country that is reserved for its own fishing vessels. Ships from other nations are excluded from a nation's fishing zone.
Fish stocks The amount of fish of particular kinds in the ocean. Fish stocks of many species are so low that some are in danger of extinction.
Fishwives Women who sold fish in markets or on the street.
Flatfish Fish, such as flounder and sole, that lie on the seabed. Both eyes are on one side of their flattened body.
Gill nets Curtainlike nets that trap fish by the gills; used to catch species that swim near the surface.
Harpoons Spearlike weapons with a rope attached that were used to catch whales.
Houseboats Boats made or fitted for habitation.

Igloo Dome-shaped Inuit house made of snow.
Intensive methods Methods used on fish farms to produce more fish in a small area.
Introduced species Nonnative animal or plant that is brought accidentally or deliberately to a new area. The effect the newcomer will have is unknown and can be devastating.
Irrigation The supply of water to the land, often by the use of canals.
Ivory The tusks of elephants and walruses are made of this hard, white substance.
Junk Traditional sailing craft of China; made of wood and bamboo with sails that look like window blinds.
Kayak One-person Inuit canoe.
Livestock Animals kept for use or sale.
Lobster pot Basket trap set to catch lobsters, which enter the pot to get the bait and cannot get out again.
Mammals Animals, ranging from mice to humans, that are generally hairy, give birth to live young, and feed them on their milk. Most mammals live on land. Whales and dolphins are mammals that live in the sea.
Mashwas Fishing boats of the Indian Ocean.
Mechanization The use of machines to do jobs that were formerly done by humans.
Mollusks Animals such as oysters, clams, and mussels that have soft bodies and sometimes hard shells. Octopuses and squid are mollusks.
Navigator The person in charge of the course a ship takes.
Offshore waters Offshore waters are beyond the coastal waters of a country.

Outboard motors Motors attached to the outside of small boats to power them.
Outrigger canoes Canoes with a wooden framework built out from the sides to stabilize them.
Overfishing A serious problem affecting fish stocks. When too many fish are taken from one area, not enough are left behind to breed and rebuild the population.
Oyster beds Places on the seabed where oysters breed.
Pearls Jewels formed inside an oyster when a grain of sand or other foreign body irritates the animal and cause it to make nacre (mother-of-pearl). It covers the offending grain to make it smooth.
Pollution Fouling of land, air, or water by artificial substances such as chemicals.
Potlatches Native American social gatherings at which gifts were given to show the giver's social status.
Processed fish Fish that is preserved in some way, such as by freezing, smoking, drying, or canning.
Protein An essential part of our diet. It is present in all living cells.
Purse net Net shaped like a pouch. The neck is drawn together to trap fish.
Quotas Amounts of fish that international regulations allow individual nations to land each year.
Radar Radiolocation system that uses radio beams to locate fish or underwater objects such as rocks.
Rafts Flat structures that float, often made from pieces of timber lashed together.
Refrigeration facilities These allow fish to be frozen on board ship. A freezer trawler can hold 800 tons of fish.

Sampans Small oriental fishing boats, usually with oars at the stern.
Schooner Wooden sailing ships with two or more masts.
Seine net Another name for a purse net.
Settlers People who move to a new country or new area of a country and set up a colony.
Shallow-water fishing Fishing undertaken around the edges of the continents where most fish are found. Deep-sea fishing takes place where the continental shelf ends, and the land slopes down to the abyss.
Skipper The captain of a fishing boat, often the owner.
Snare To trap, or snare, fish in a snare.
Sonar Echo-sounding device that uses sound signals to locate shoals of fish.
Spawn Fish breed, or spawn, by laying eggs. Some fish, such as salmon, return each year to the same spawning grounds.
Species Kind of animal or plant.
Sponges "Colonial" underwater animals with porous skeletons. We use the skeletons of dead sponges for washing and cleaning.
Tackle Hooks, lines, and other equipment needed for fishing.
Totem poles Poles on which Native Americans carved emblems (totems) of gods or beasts that they revered.
Trawl Bag-shaped net pulled through water to catch middle-water and bottom-living fish.
Trawler Fishing boat used to lay trawl nets. There are two main kinds: side trawlers and stern trawlers.
Trolling vessels Boats that trail fishing lines behind them.
Umiak Inuit boat made of wood and sealskin, usually rowed by women.
Wet fish Fresh, unprocessed fish traditionally sold from a marble slab and hosed down with water.
Whalers Whaling ships or the people who man them.

Index

Air-sea search 11, *11*
Alewife 43
Anglers 41
Aral Sea 42, *42*
Auctions 18, *19*, 20

Bait *13*, 25
Balance of nature 42
Bass 32
Boat people 36-37, *36*
Bream 32
Breeding season 30

Canals 42
Candlefish 30
Canning and canneries 12, 23, 31, 39
Canoes 6, 10
    seagoing 31, 36
Charter boats *35*
Chinook 30
Clambake 17, *17*
Clams 14, 17, *17*
Cod 13, 14, 21, 26
    Sacred 25
Cod war 27
Colonists 24
Commerical catchers 35
Communal fisheries 6-10, *8*, 22, 23, 28-29, *28*, 38-39
Consumer 35
Consumer goods 27
Crabs 6, 14, 34
Crawfish 17, 33, *33*
Crustaceans 14
Cultured pearls 34
Customs and beliefs 8-9

Deckhands 26
Deep-sea fishing 26, 36
Diesel engines 10
Dories *24*, 25
Drying 6, *16*, 24, *28*
Dutch auction 20

Echolocation 14
Ecological disasters 42, *42*, 43
Economy 11, 39
    tourism and 40-41
Exporting 39

Factory ship 11, 14, 16, 18, 20
Family business 6, 8
Fertilizer 24, 32
Fish baskets 6, 9
Fish farm 21, 22, 23, 33, *33*, 34, 45, *45*
    intensive methods 45

Fish festivities 17, 33
Fishhooks, making 6
Fishing community 6-10
    destruction of 37, 40, 42
    in the 21st century 45
Fishing disputes 11
Fishing fleet: blessing 9
    loss of 8
    pay 26
Fishing grounds 21
    see also Grand Banks; Gulf of Mexico
Fishing limits 26, 43-44
Fishing methods 12-13
Fish lore 8-9, *8-9*
Fish markets 18-20, *18*, 41
Fishmonger 34
Fish stocks 21
    effects of overfishing 11, 22-23
    preserving 43
Fish traps 6, 38
    see also Rivers
Fishwives *19*
Flatfish 14
Flounder 14, 21
Food fish 13, 23, 26, 32
    raw 34
Freezing *26*
Freshwater fish 14, 21, 32

Gill nets 13, *13*
Grand Banks 9, 12, 21, *24*, 25
Gulf of Mexico 22, 32

Haddock 13
Halibut 14, 30
Hand nets 10
Harpoons 10
Herring 13, 14, 21, 30
Houseboats 36, 37
Hurricanes 32

Igloo 29
Introduced species 39, *39*, 42
Inuit 22, 28-29, *28-29*
Irrigation 42
Ivory and bone 29

Junk 36, *36*

Kayak 28, *28*, 29

Lake fishing 14, 22, 23, 32, 38-39, *38-39*
Lake Victoria 39
Lines 6, 12, *12*
Lobster pot *13*, 32
Lobsters 6, 13, 14, 21, 32

Mackerel 13, 14, 32, 34
Mammals
    see Whales
Mashwas 36
Mechanization 11
Menhaden 32
Mollusks 14
Mullet 32
Mussels 13, 14

Navigator 26
Nets 6, 9, *11*, 13, *13*, 15, 28, 38
    controls on 43
    Native American methods 24
Nile perch 39, *39*
North Atlantic 11
North Sea 26-27

Offshore waters
    controls on 43
Outboard motors 10
Outrigger canoes 36
Overfishing 11, *21*, 22-23, 27, 36-37, 43
Oyster beds 34
Oysters 6, 13, 17

Pearls 34, *34-35*
Peru Current 22
Pollack 21
Pollution 11, 36, 42, 43
Potlatches *30*, 31
Prawns 14
Preparing and preserving 6, 13, 16, 18
Processed fish 16, 32
Protein 13
Purse net 13, *13*
    see also Seine net

Quotas 26

Radar 14
Radio contact 11
Rafts 6
Red snapper 32
Reed boats 7
Refrigeration facilities 15
Ring net 35
Rivers: nets across 14, 39
    traps in 6, 30, *31*, 38
Ropes 6

Safety at sea 8, 11, *11*, 26
Sailing boats 6
Sails 6
Salmon 13, 30, *30*, 34

Salting 6, 24
Saltwater fish 14
Sampans 36
Sardines 13, 14, 34
Schooner *24*, 25
Sea gods 8, 9, 10
Sea snakes, venomous *14*
Seine net 13, *13*
    see also Purse net
Shallow-water fishing 36
Shark 32
Shellfish 6, 13, 14, 21, 32, 36
Shrimps 13, 14, 32, *32*
Side trawlers 13
Skipper 14, 18, 26
Slaves 31
Smoking fish 6, 39
Snare 24, 32
Sonar 14
Sorting the catch 15
Spawn 30, *30*
Species 13
Sponges 32, *32*
Sports fishing *35*, 41
Squid 14, 34
Stern trawlers 13, *13*
Storms 8, 11

Tackle
    shops 41
Tlingit 30
Totem poles 30, *30*
Tourist industry 40-41, *44*, 45
Transporting preserved fish 24
Trawler 26
    hauling in the catch 15
    loss of 11
Trawl net 13, *13*, 32
Trolling 35
Tropical fish 14
Trout 14, 45
    freshwater 32
    sea 32
Tuna 13, 14, 32, 34, 35
Tuna hunters 35, *35*
Types of fish 14

Umiak 28

"Wall of death" fishing 13, *13*
Weather forecasting 8, 11
Wet fish *26*
Whales 20, *20*, *28*, 30
Whiting 21
Wildlife, dangers to 13, *13*
Winches 15
World fish catch 22, *22*, 34

Copyright © Cherrytree Press Ltd 1992